Stedmon Makes Me Laugh and I Make Him Pray

by Barbara Bryant

Copyright © BARBARA BRYANT

Stedmon Makes Me Laugh and I Make Him Pray
by Barbara Bryant

Printed in the United States of America

ISBN 9781619960060

All rights reserved solely by the author. The author guarantees all contents are original and do not infringe upon the legal rights of any other person or work. No part of this book may be reproduced in any form without the permission of the author. The views expressed in this book are not necessarily those of the publisher.

www.xulonpress.com

Introduction

Author and Speaker Barbara Bryant has many wonderful memories of her boys as children and wants to share them with you. Typically, children are funny and often make us smile. So it was with Steven and Stedmon who were ten years apart in age. Enjoy!

CONTENTS

Chapter One
Stop Looking At Me 9

Chapter Two
The Water Tried To Make Me Die 13

Chapter Three
Rock a Bye Baby 17

Chapter Four
Talking to Jesus--Again 23

Chapter Five
Too Much Soda Pop 26

Chapter Six
Growing up 31

Chapter Seven
Puppy Love 36

Chapter Eight
The Imagination Station.. 42

Chapter Nine
Clothes Make the Man 46

Post Script
In the End 49

ONE

Stop Looking at Me

It had been a long week, and I was exhausted, so looking forward to a restful Saturday morning with nothing pressing to do. The boys and I were at home in Southern California, still in our pajamas. A fire burned in the family room hearth warming the house, and I had curled up on the sofa to relax, listening to the comforting sound of rain on the roof.

The boys were in their rooms down a short hallway. At age fourteen, Steven was very musically gifted, and with a new keyboard I knew he would spend all day teaching himself to play. His room was a typical teen boy's room with a Lakers' spread covering his full-sized bed and their posters decorating the walls. On the floor was a colorful rug displaying musical notes with the proverbial pile of dirty clothes not far away. Against the wall a desk sat cluttered with unfinished schoolwork. Steven's disposition was very laid back. In fact, he was one of those children who had to be told many times before he accomplished an assigned task like cleaning his room or finishing his homework. He loved his room, with one major exception. A long, tunnel-like closet connected his room with the one occupied by his four-year old brother, Stedmon.

Stedmon's room was a four-year-old's dream, with Disney characters covering the walls. He loved playing in his bunk bed/playhouse, but hated to sleep in the bed. The rest of the space was filled with play drums, a basketball court and tons of toys piled in the middle of the room.

At age four, Stedmon loved Steven and his room, and couldn't seem to get enough of his company. And the tunnel-like closet offered frequent and easy access to Steven's room, much to his delight. That particular day he had made a game of going in and out of Steven's room through the closet, and his brother had finally had enough. He had banished Stedmon from his room, but that wasn't the end of the story.

From the family room down the hall I heard Stedmon's plaintive call.

"Mom . . ."

"Yes, Stedmon."

"Steven keeps looking at me."

"It's okay, Stedmon. Steven can look at you."

"I don't want Steven to look at me. Can you tell him to stop? He's aggravating me."

"Steven, can you stop looking at your brother?"

Steven was clearly annoyed. "Mom, how can I stop looking at him when he's sitting on the floor of my room looking directly at me?"

Stedmon said, "No, I'm not. I'm looking at your keyboard."

"Come on you guys. I'm trying to rest. Steven, just don't look at him."

Not ten seconds later Stedmon repeated, "Mom, Steven's looking at me again."

I sighed aloud. "That's enough. It's okay for your brother to look at you. He likes you. Big brothers always look at their little brothers. All right?"

"All right."

"Now go play with your toys until lunch time."

At that instant the silence was punctuated by Stedmon's piercing scream. "Mom!"

"What is it now?"

"Steven is looking at me again."

"Steven! Stedmon! Both of you come here right now!"

They appeared before me, both upset and looking guilty. I said, "Steven, what are you doing to your brother?"

"Nothing, Mom. He's been bugging me all day going back and forth through the closet. He's driving me crazy. The last time he came into my room, he sat on the floor and looked at me to see if I was looking at him."

"Okay, now that's enough. This is silly. Stedmon?"

"Yes, Mom."

"I want you to stop looking at Steven. Do you hear me?"

He sighed. "Yes, Mom."

"Steven, stop looking at Stedmon, okay?"

"But Mom, I'm not doing anything. He's the one bothering me."

"Okay, that's it. I've had it. Nobody is to look at anyone else until I finish my nap. Do you both hear me?"

"Yes, Mom," said Steven.

"Mom . . ."

"What is it now, Stedmon?"

He tilted his head and gave me a clever grin. "You said we weren't supposed to look at each other, but you're looking at me right now."

"That's it, Stedmon. Go to your room and don't come out until you talk to Jesus."

Stedmon's Prayer

"Dear Jesus, I think Steven should work on not looking at me. Mom said she was going to the gym today, but she spent the whole day watching TV on the couch. Steven told Mom he didn't have any cookies today, but I caught him stuffing three cookies in his mouth while Mom was sleeping. Dear Jesus, everybody did the wrong thing today, but I'm the only one who has to sit in my room and pray. Can you tell God that my Mom and brother are in big trouble with you?"

"Stedmon!"

"Yes, Mom."

"I can hear you!"

"Sorry, Mom."

In a low tone a now much humbler Stedmon resumed his prayer: "Dear Jesus. I promise not to look at Steven for the rest of the day. Amen."

A Mom's Perspective

"Dear God, I often laugh at the silly things I see Stedmon do. And while the things that bother my son seem trivial to me I know they're very important to him. Sometimes when he acts that way I just want to snatch him up and lock him in his room until he's old enough for college. But he is so funny.

The other day at the store, he asked a perfect stranger, "Are you pregnant, or are you just fat?" Thank heaven she was pregnant. Though it was an awkward moment all I could do was laugh. And while I sometimes get upset when he repeatedly says things like: "Steven keeps looking at me," I need to remember that he is still a child and will not always think logically or behave perfectly. Help me to thoughtfully choose my battles today in order to save my sanity. Help me focus on the important behaviors You want to see change in his life and prayerfully decide what lesser ones You want me to address. I praise You for wisdom and pray that Stedmon quickly exits this stage of development."

TWO

The Water Tried To Make Me Die

Stedmon was two, and Steven twelve when we spent five days' vacation at the Wyndham Hotel in Palm Springs, California. It was a very hot July with midday temperatures soaring into the 100s. It was too hot to do many outdoor activities, so we spent much of our time indoors, shopping, going to movies and playing games at the arcades. We would wait until temps cooled down in the evening to do much running around.

One very hot day Stedmon was anxious to swim in the pool. Because he loved bath time he saw the pool as little more than a big bathtub. He was less than three feet tall and had not yet learned to swim when I gave him strict instructions to wait until Mom could accompany him into the four-foot deep water. Of course I had no idea what happened when the boys were alone.

While sitting out at the pool with Stedmon, Steven urged him to jump in the water telling him it was just like the bathtub at home. Believing his brother would never steer him wrong Stedmon jumped in without supervision and without our permission.

Suddenly Steven called, "Mom, Stedmon jumped in the water!" Steven laughed as he watched me jump in the swimming pool and pull Stedmon out. And while Stedmon was over his head, unable to swim and about to drown, he too was laughing, jumping up and down to keep his head above water. I was terrified seeing water over the level of his nose and mouth, but he wasn't afraid at all. Once he was safely on the edge of the pool, he said, "That was fun! Let's do it again." I shook my head. "Stedmon, you can't do that. You almost drowned. You can't swim in four feet of water. The water is too deep."

Stedmon argued, "Yes, I can."

I could hear Steven laughing in the distance.

I turned towards Steven and said, "Listen, Steven, you need to keep an eye on your brother while I go out and get lunch, and don't let him go in the water until I return."

Unknown to me, while I was away Steven gave his brother permission to go into the shallow water but no farther. Steven went so far as to ask, "Do you promise not to tell?"

"Yes" said Stedmon.

"Okay, but you only have ten minutes so hurry."

Stedmon was thrilled and jumped in. But while Steven was distracted Stedmon decided to go into deeper water where he lost his balance and began to struggle and scream for help. A lifeguard ended up jumping in to pull him out. Steven promised Stedmon a quarter when they returned to the hotel room, if he agreed not to tell Mom. Stedmon was still crying when he agreed not to tell.

When I returned with the food I was surprised to see the boys sitting quietly in the patio chairs beside the pool. To this day, Stedmon, like a whirling dervish, is never still. It was clear that he was not eager to get into the water. Later when I invited him to go swimming, Stedmon said, "I don't want to swim now. I want to go back to the hotel room." As we were walking to the room Stedmon broke down and said, "The water tried to make me die."

I said, "What?"

"The water tried to make me die."

"How did the water try to make you die?"

"Well, Steven told me to jump in the pool, and the water tried to make me die."

By that time, Steven had returned to the room to hear me explain, "He says the water tried to make him die."

Stedmon Makes Me Laugh and I Make Him Pray

Steven tried unsuccessfully to hide his laughter, which only made Stedmon cry harder. When I saw how upset he was I sat on the bed, pulled him onto my lap and hugged him. "I'm sorry the water tried to make you die. But God wanted you to live, which is why you're still here." Then I asked, "Why were you in the water, when I told you not to get in unless I was with you?'

He replied, "Steven told me I could get in if I stayed in the kids' section."

Steven interrupted, "But he moved to the deeper water when I wasn't looking. He didn't listen to me."

Stedmon screamed, "I was in the kids' section."

Steven interrupted, still laughing, "No you weren't. You moved to where it was three and a half feet deep."

I frowned. "Well, you're both in trouble now."

At that point Stedmon stopped crying and said, "Steven, can I have my quarter now?"

Steven shook his head. "No, because you told on me."

"No I didn't. I just said to myself *the water made me die*, and Mom heard me."

Steven turned to look at me. "Mom?"

"Yes, son."

"Stedmon is fibbing again."

I gave Stedmon the look. "Stedmon, do you want to call on Jesus in the middle of the day?"

"No, Mom, but Steven should."

Stedmon's Prayer

"Dear Jesus, I'm really glad Steven got into trouble today. Usually it's only me who gets in trouble. So thanks for helping me out today. We should do this again some time. Amen."

A Mother's Perspective

While it sounded funny when Stedmon said the water tried to make him die, it wasn't long before the whole story came out and I realized how close he had actually come to drowning. It was time for a serious conversation about the need for obedience. My boys needed to learn that God has no obligation to protect us when we move out from under His protection, in disobedience. It was a lesson none of us would soon forget. However, to this day we still tease Stedmon about the phrase ... "the water tried to make me die."

THREE

Rock a Bye Baby

From the time Stedmon was born he was very ill with allergies and asthma, even though I breastfed him. And because I wasn't working at that time I was able to establish a bedtime routine of bathing then feeding him, before we would both drop off to sleep in my bed.

By the time he was a year old I tried to put him to bed in his crib, but he would cry inconsolably and wake his brother from a sound sleep, when he had to get up to go to school in the morning. As mothers do I always took pity on him and would rock him to sleep then put him in my bed just to keep the peace.

When he was three years old my sister Cynthia said she felt Stedmon was manipulating me. At her house he slept with her boys, and if that was possible it was also possible for him to sleep without his mother, in his own bed.

One night at dinner I had served Stedmon's favorite food, macaroni and cheese, when I said to Stedmon, "Listen, Stedmon. Tonight you have to sleep in your own bed. Okay?"

Stedmon agreed, but when it came time to go to bed he screamed uncontrollably without end, until I finally gave up and put him in bed with me. I tried for three successive nights, but had no luck breaking the cycle. My mother (who has nine children; I am the youngest) happened by on day four.

It was that time again.

"Time to go to bed, Stedmon." But he was nowhere to be found. After an extensive search I finally found him.

"Stedmon, why are you hiding under the blanket in your brother's bed?"

"I can't sleep in my room by myself."

"Yes, you can."

"No I can't!"

Steven called out, "Hip, hip, hooray! Finally, you are going to make him sleep in his own bed."

The door bell rang and I motioned my mother inside. "Mom, I'm glad to see you. I need your help. I can't get Stedmon to sleep in his bed."

"What do you mean, you can't get his little butt to sleep in his bed? Who's in charge here anyway?"

Steven smiled and waved. "Hi, Granny."

"Hi, Baby. How come you all can't get Stedmon to sleep in his bedroom?"

Steven turned to look at me. "It's Mom's fault. Ever since he was a baby, she's rocked him to sleep every night and let him sleep with her, and now he won't go to sleep in his bedroom. If she put him in her bed, he goes to sleep. And if she put him in my bed, he'll go to sleep, but if we put him in his room, he wakes up and screams at the top of his lungs, and Mom is a big softy who can't stand to let him cry. For years she's been running to his rescue and putting him back in her bed or in bed with me. Now, he's four years old and she is trying to make him sleep in his bed."

With the authority of a good mother, Mom said, "You need to establish a memorable bedtime routine. The routine need not be elaborate, but it should be something he looks forward to each night. It can be as simple as reading a favorite book in a special part of the room or watching a movie while lying in his bed."

Suddenly she turned and called out, "Stedmon!"

"Yes, Granny."

"Why won't you sleep in your own bed?"

Stedmon flashed her, his best pout. "Steven won't let me sleep in his bed."

"That's not what I asked. Why won't you sleep in your bed?"

"Granny! Steven won't let me sleep in his bed!"

"Barbara! What time is Stedmon's bedtime?"

"He goes to bed at eight o'clock."

"Stedmon?"

At that moment he knew his number was up. "Yes, Granny."

"You and I are going to do something special tonight. We are going to curl up on your bed and watch one of your favorite movies. Go move all the toys off your bed so we can snuggle up together."

"Okay, Granny. Can I have a Popsicle too?"

"Yes, you can."

I said, "What are you up to, Mom?"

Mom took me aside and spoke in a low tone. "Well, you said he normally falls asleep when watching television. So if you let him watch a movie in his bed, then he'll fall asleep there."

Steven smiled. "That's a good trick, Granny."

Granny turned on the television in Stedmon's room and put a movie in the VCR. They crawled into his bed and rested their heads on his pillow. Within thirty minutes he was fast asleep.

Not long afterward Granny exited his room and called out softly, "Barbara! Praise God! He's asleep. Just let him watch his favorite movie in his bed each night and he'll fall asleep right where he's supposed to be."

Even Steven couldn't stifle his relief. "Thanks a lot, Granny. I can't believe he's finally sleeping in his own bed."

I sighed aloud. "I can't believe it was that easy. Leave it to Granny to figure it out."

The phone rang a short time later. Steven said, "It's probably Granny letting us know she made it home." It was Mom, but she asked to talk to Steven.

Stedmon Makes Me Laugh and I Make Him Pray

When he picked up the phone she said, "A penny for your thoughts."

"Well, I was just thinking how great it will be when I get to sleep in my bed all by myself tonight. I was tired of Stedmon sleeping with me. Thanks Granny."

"Enjoy your time alone," said Mom, "and thanks for being so patient with your little brother. You know, I think you deserve a night at Pizza Hut tomorrow."

Steven smiled. "Fast food during the week? Cool."

At two a.m. the house was dark and still when terrified screams broke the silence. Stedmon yelled, "Mom! Mom! Mom!" I leaped out of the bed and ran to the rescue.

"What's wrong?"

"There's a monster in my room."

"Where?"

"In my closet."

I opened the closet door. Playing along I picked up Stedmon's bat and started hitting the imaginary monster in the closet.

Steven was standing in the doorway watching. "You can go back to sleep now, Stedmon, since Mom killed the monster."

He shook his head, clearly unconvinced. "But there's another one under my bed."

I began hitting an imaginary monster under the bed.

I said, "Where is he getting the idea there are monsters in the closet?" After a pause I added, "Hmm . . .I wonder--what movie did he watch with my mom?" I walked over to the VCR and ejected the movie. I shook my head. Of course he had nightmares about monsters. They had watched "Monsters Incorporated" a Disney movie about monsters living in the closet. My mom had let him watch the wrong movie.

"Can I sleep with Steven?" asked Stedmon.

By then Steven was back in his room. He said, "Listen Sted, everybody else in your daycare class sleeps in their own room."

Stedmon shook his head. "I know one who doesn't."

Steven frowned. "Who?"

Stedmon flashed a clever grin. "Me."

I looked at Steven trying not to laugh.

Steven said, "Stedmon, Mom just killed all the monsters, so you can go back to sleep in your own bed now."

As was his custom Stedmon burst into tears. To calm him down, I put him in the bed with Steven.

I couldn't stifle a sigh. "Listen Stedmon. You and I need to talk about this in the morning."

"Yes, Mom."

Stedmon's Prayer (the next morning)

"Dear Jesus, I am not to come out of my room until we talk. Do you have something to say to me? Mom told me I'm not supposed to fib when I pray, so here's the truth. I do not want to sleep in my bedroom because I like Steven's room better. My big brother is really cool. He has a keyboard, a guitar and drums in his room. All I have in my room is toys for kids, but I'm not a kid. Mom said you answer prayers, so can you answer my prayer by eight tonight because that's my bedtime."

A Mother's Thoughts

"Dear God, I have come to the conclusion that Stedmon does not have insomnia. He is just bent on sleeping in his big brother's room. It's clear that we'll have to discuss why it's wrong to manipulate someone, and why God doesn't like it. But when I listened to him pray this morning I was amazed to hear how he is learning to talk to you so freely. Although his prayers are hilarious, they are also sincere and honest. I am going to answer his prayer by letting him sleep in Steven's room tonight. That will build his faith and make him believe that you do really answer a kid's prayer and that you care about his concerns. Help me to be tougher tomorrow night, okay? Thank you for wisdom in raising this amazing child. Although you have entrusted him to me, I know he really belongs to You. Remove the fear in his life, in Jesus name, Amen.

It was amazing to see Stedmon sleeping in his bed one month later. I'm glad I was patient with my son.

FOUR

Talking To Jesus –Again!

When Stedmon was three, I begin to interpret his behavior as manipulation. One evening during bath time, his actions really triggered feelings of "That's the last straw!" It was time to set limits.

One day I was bathing Stedmon and he asked me to sing his favorite song. Unsure which song he referred to I ran through all the children's worship songs I could remember. But over and over he would cry out, very upset, "No, Mom, that's not my song. Sing my song!"

He was so upset that he thrashed around in the tub, and I was afraid he would injure himself, so I felt desperate to come up with the correct song. Steven even sat beside the tub and joined in singing every children's song he could think of. But as hard as we tried we couldn't come up with 'his song.'

Soon he was weeping uncontrollably and nearly inconsolable when Dad walked inside wanting to know what the ruckus was about.

"He's upset because he wants me to sing his song, but I can't figure out what it is. Do you know what his song is?"

Dad smiled. "Of course." And he began to dance and do the motions, as he sang the "Sponge Bob" theme song. "Who lives in a pineapple under the sea?" And Stedmon sang, "SpongeBob SquarePants!" Instantly Stedmon's tears turned to joy as he happily sang along. I was floored.

To Dad I said, "Where did you learn that?"

"What do you think we watch when it's his hour to watch his favorite show on television? I have to sit there and endure all these crazy kid shows."

The next evening during bath time, I started singing the "Sponge Bob" theme song, and Stedmon began to cry.

I asked, "What's wrong, honey?"

"That's not my song."

"What you mean that's not your song?"

Very upset he shouted, "That's not my song!" As it turned out he had a new song that night. In fact, I noticed he began to frequently use those kinds of situations to become very upset and throw his weight around. I realized that he had developed an attitude problem that I needed to confront.

The next time it happened I said, "Stop that right now, Stedmon. You and I are going to have a little talk."

"Am I in trouble, Mom?"

"You are."

"What did I do now?"

"You have your own sort of little tantrum, letting your emotions get out of control, so that you can't even choose to calm yourself down when you need to."

"Sorry, Mom. Should I pray now?"

"Wait until you're out of the tub and then talk to Jesus about it."

Stedmon's Prayer

"Jesus, Mom told me to talk to you again, because I'm in trouble, but I'm not sure how to change what I did wrong. I guess you need to show me and help me be a good boy, instead of getting out of control." To me he shouted, "Is that good enough, Mom?"

"Good enough, Stedmon." Stedmon finished, "She said it's okay, so amen."

A Mother's Thoughts

Over the years Stedmon got into many scrapes and was told to go talk to Jesus. And while those incidents might seem funny, they actually motivated him to admit when he was wrong and listen to what God had to say. When we think our children are too small to understand, God has a way of speaking right to their spirits. Thank you, Lord, for breaking through to my little boy when no one else can.

FIVE

Too Much Soda Pop

One Sunday after church we joined my sister Cynthia and her husband Tom, sons, Jerame, age twelve, and Thomas, age eleven, for dinner at the Sizzler Restaurant in Bellflower, California. Her boys treat my sons more like brothers than cousins. The adults sat on one end of the table visiting while the children sat together at the other.

"Whose drink is this?" Stedmon asked his cousins Thomas and Jerame.

Jerame said, "It's your brother's soda pop, so you'd better not drink it."

Stedmon asked, "Where did he go?"

Thomas said, "He went to the bathroom to wash his hands."

Stedmon turned to his uncle. "Uncle Tom, can I have some of Steven's soda pop?"

Tom said, "Did Steven say you could have a drink?"

"Yes."

"Okay Stedmon, just have a little bit."

I protested. "Tom, don't let Stedmon drink soda. He'll have to use the restroom."

He waved off my concerns. "He'll be all right. I'll take him to the restroom when he needs to go."

I shook my head. "That's not the problem. He won't tell you he has to go until the last minute and will end up wetting his clothes."

Stedmon Makes Me Laugh and I Make Him Pray

Tom waved off my concerns. "Don't worry. He'll be all right."

Steven returned from the restroom, sat down and frowned. "Who drank my soda?"

Stedmon shouted, "Thomas did it!"

Steven hailed the waitress. "Excuse me, Miss. May I have a refill?"

"Of course. What were you drinking?"

"Strawberry soda."

The waitress refilled Steven's drink while he chatted with Thomas and Jerame. But while he was distracted, Stedmon began drinking the refill and drank it until it was gone.

I instantly noticed the odd, telltale signs of urgency. "Tom, Stedmon is fidgeting at the table, which means he needs to go to the restroom."

Tom said, "Hey Stedmon. Do you need to go to the restroom?"

"No."

I argued, knowing the consequences. "Yes, he does, Tom. I know what that fidgeting means. Ask him again."

"Do you need to go to the restroom, man?"

"No, Uncle Tom."

Suddenly Steven noticed his empty soda glass. "Ahh! Who drank my soda?"

Once again Stedmon pointed at Thomas. "He did it."

"No, I didn't. Stedmon drank both drinks, and he's fidgeting because he needs to go to the bathroom."

Stedmon was resolute. "No, I don't."

Steven's eyes grew wide with annoyance. "Mom! Stedmon is fibbing again."

But it was already too late. I shouted, "Oh oh! Tom, get Stedmon. He's wetting his pants."

Without missing a beat, Stedmon screeched, "Uncle Tom, Steven spilled his soda on my clothes."

Steven rolled his eyes. "I did no such thing. He's peeing on himself."

Tom rushed to grab Stedmon and ran toward the restroom, but it was already far too late. By the time they arrived his uncle's clothes were also drenched.

In the privacy of the restroom Tom sighed aloud and studied his nephew's face. "Didn't I ask if you had to use the restroom?"

"You did, but I didn't have to go then. I have to use it now, but I didn't know until it was too late."

After a pause Stedmon begged, "Please! Please! Don't tell Mom."

"I won't, but you will. Go tell her you wet your pants."

Tom and Stedmon walked back to the table where I was sitting.

Without missing a beat Stedmon confessed, "Mom, Steven wet my pants."

I frowned. "Stedmon! Are you telling the truth about who wet your pants? I told you what happens when you're dishonest. Now let me ask you again--did you wet your pants?"

"No, Uncle Tom was moving me real fast to the restroom, but it wasn't fast enough."

I turned to my sister Cynthia. "Cynthia, I am going to have to do something about this problem. He's four years old and not only does he still wet his pants, but he refuses to own up to it. He always has a reason—an excuse for all his actions."

I frowned at Stedmon. "As soon as we get home you will go to your room and talk to Jesus. Do you hear me?"

"Yes, Mom."

Stedmon didn't want to wait. "Dear God . . ."

"I said wait until you get home."

He argued, "But you said Jesus was everywhere."

"He is, but I still want you to wait until you get home." Looking up to heaven I sighed. "Lord, give me strength with this boy."

Stedmon's Prayer (later that night)

"Dear God, I told a fib today. Sorry for drinking Steven's soda and sorry for getting in trouble with Mom. Can you let Steven get in trouble next time? He told me I wasn't a Christian because I fib too much. I told him if that was the case than he's not a Christian either. I know because he said no when Mom asked him if he was talking on the phone while she was at the store yesterday. He paid me a quarter to keep quiet. Since I'm no longer going to be a fibber, I am going to tell Mom about the quarter Steven gave me so he can get in trouble, too."

"Mom!"

"What is it, Stedmon?"

"I want to give you this quarter."

I cocked my head to study his face. "Where did you get a quarter?"

"Steven gave it to me."

"Why would he do that?"

"So I wouldn't tell you he was on the telephone while you were at the store last night. I also know he put his dirty clothes under his bed because I helped him. And he did not water the grass in the backyard the way he said he did. He also paid me a quarter . . ."

"Steven! Come here right now . . ."

A Mother's Thoughts

"Dear God, I once again had to laugh at the antics of my youngest son, Stedmon. You and I both knew he would wet his pants after drinking too much soda. But it was funny watching him drink that soda, fidget and deny that he had to go, with no clue that he would soon wet himself in front of everyone. And while I couldn't help but laugh his lies really are a problem we must deal with. This week I want to talk to him about values and how important it is to tell the truth. Please give me wisdom and give him ears to hear your Spirit on the subject. Help me to train him to be a young man of integrity and honesty starting now. Amen!"

SIX

Growing Up

Stedmon had been looking forward to kindergarten with great anticipation. He continually talked about going to "Steven's school." There was no way to convince him that, though Steven had attended there, he had already moved on to middle school.

Stedmon stood smiling, seeing all his things laid out for school, at the foot of his bed. His clothes. His shoes. Even the new backpack I had ordered from a catalog. It was striking, displaying a vivid red Spiderman in motion on the front, and Stedmon's name stenciled in white letters on the back.

He reached down and picked it up holding it to his tummy. He could scarcely contain his excitement over his first day of school.

Without warning he called out, "Steven, come here!"

Steven appeared in his doorway. "What?"

"I get to go to school with you today!"

Steven shook his head. "No. You're going to my old school. But you'll have a lot of fun there. Let the teachers know you're my little brother, okay?"

"Okay."

"Will I get to play with toys?"

Steven frowned and shook his head. "No. The teachers are mean and make you read all day long."

I overheard their conversation and sighed. "Steven! Stop telling fibs to your brother."

"I'm just playing with him."

Stedmon kicked Steven in the leg for fibbing and ran to his bedroom.

Steven had had enough. "Mom, he just kicked me."

"Well, you shouldn't have told him that. You guys hurry up and get dressed. Breakfast is almost ready."

"Steven!"

"What is it now?"

"Can you walk me to my class?"

"I can't, because my school starts earlier than yours. But listen, you'll be fine. You'll meet lots of new boys and girls your age. You're going to love it. Just don't be bossy like you are at home."

Stedmon made a face. "I'm not bossy."

"Yes, you are."

"Okay boys. It's time to go. Let's pray. Stedmon, why don't you lead the prayer today?"

He shook his head. "Make Steven do it."

I sighed, knowing we were running late. "Steven, will you pray, so we can go?"

"How come you won't make Stedmon pray? You told him to do it first."

"Do you guys have to fuss about everything? I'll pray. Dear Lord, watch over my sons today while they are at school. Protect us all, in Jesus name. Amen."

Turning to the boys I said, "Let's go."

On the way to the car I asked Stedmon, "So how do you feel about kindergarten? Are you excited?"

He nodded. "Yes. Do I get to play?"

"You sure do. Your day will be filled with games, naps and snacks, and you'll get to meet lots of new friends your age."

Elementary School

Although I was struggling to know my baby was growing up I was confident that the Elementary School would balance a warm and nurturing atmosphere with high academic expectations. Steven had

attended there so I knew it was an excellent learning environment that also encouraged children to develop both integrity and good character. It was a mid-sized school, with twenty-two teachers and a total of 407 students, including fifty-two kindergarteners.

The classroom was already filled with happy, noisy children when we arrived. We met his teacher, whom he liked right away. Then we located Stedmon's assigned seat, which was located close to the teacher's desk.

He had already made up his mind that it was going to be a good day. "Mom, I am going to have a lot of fun today. You can go home now."

As I wiped away tears I said, "Stedmon, Mom is both happy and sad today."

He turned to frown at me, clearly unable to understand. "Why Mom?"

"Because my baby boy is growing up--starting kindergarten today. Do you want me to stay with you for a little while on your first day?"

He shook his head. "No, Mom, that would be embarrassing. Maybe you can go to Steven's school and stay with him."

"All right, honey. I'm leaving. Obey the teacher. No exceptions!"

As I drove home I felt both sad and excited; I couldn't help but hope he would do well.

At the end of the day I drove to school to pick him up.

"Hi, honey. How was school?"

"It was fun, Mom. I played on the playground and found a new best friend whose name is Brian. Here, Mom. The teacher told me to give this paper to you."

I opened the envelope and the note read: *Dear Mrs. Bryant, Stedmon had a difficult time adjusting to class today. He refused to come into class after recess. The school's guard had to physically remove him from the rocking horse and bring him into the classroom. He was kicking and screaming the entire time. He also refused to pay attention or follow directions. I did not call you about this problem because it was only his first day of school. It would help if you let him know that he cannot play the entire time at school. Thank you!*

"Stedmon!"

"Yes Mom."

"Did you have a problem at school today?"

"No, Mom, but the man did."

"What man?"

"The big man. He fell in the dirt trying to pull me off the rocking horse."

"Why did he have to pull you off the rocking horse?"

"I don't know."

We had just arrived at home when I said, "Stedmon, the teacher said you were disrespectful and refused to go inside after recess ended. The big man had to pull you off the rocking horse because you refused to obey. Is that right?"

"Yes Mom. I'm sorry. I need to talk to Jesus?"

I nodded. "Yes, you do. Go to your room right now and stay there."

Stedmon's Prayer
His door was open so I overheard his prayer.

"Dear Jesus, I have to stay in my room tonight, because I got in trouble at school. Mom told me to think about what I did and talk to you about it. I hung out with my new friends today. I dressed myself. I ate all my food at lunch time. I played on the playground for a really long time, and it was fun."

I shouted, "Stedmon!"

"Yes Mom . . ."

"Talk to God about the things you did wrong today! And do it right now."

"Yes, Mom."

"Dear Jesus. Mom and the teacher said I was disrespectful. And they were right. I refused to obey the teacher and that was not nice. I won't do it again Jesus, I promise. Jesus, Mom said it's time I live up to my potential. I don't know what potential means but it must have something to do with school. Can you help me be potential tomorrow? One more thing--now that the teacher knows I have a mother, I guess I'd better remember too, because they'll talk to each other about me. Amen!"

A Mother's Thoughts

"Dear God, I silently laughed when I found out the school security guard had to remove my five-year old son from the playground. I was at least eighteen when I saw a police officer up close and personal for the first time. At that time, I was driving my parents' car and ran a red light. Boy, was I scared. But not Stedmon. In fact, he tried to wiggle his way out of the police officer's arms. And while his behavior is perfectly normal for his developmental level, I still need to address his behavior. Give me wisdom to know how to speak to these issues, and give him ears to hear. Amen."

SEVEN

Puppy Love

S teven was fifteen and Stedmon was five when they put their heads together and came to an important decision.

One day out of the blue Stedmon said, "Mom, can me and Steven have a dog?"

I cocked my head in question. "Whose idea was it to get a dog?"

Steven admitted. "We've talked about it, and we'd both like to have a dog."

I nodded. "You probably can if you promise to take care of it."

Stedmon smiled. "Oh, we will. When can we get the dog?"

"What if we go to the dog shelter on Saturday?"

Stedmon, whose mind was like a steel trap, had to know what day it was, everyday. Every morning when he got up he ran to the calendar to see what day of the week it was. Because he still couldn't read he always screamed his brother's name at the top of his lungs, "Steven, what day is it?" That day Steven said it was Tuesday and Stedmon was satisfied with that answer. The trouble was that most of the time Steven gave him incorrect answers. He seemed to get a big kick out of giving his little brother wrong information. Stedmon was none the wiser until I intervened.

Stedmon screamed back to Steven, "How long will it be before Saturday?" Steven chuckled and said, "Tomorrow

Stedmon Makes Me Laugh and I Make Him Pray

is Saturday. Try to remember that Saturday comes after Tuesday."

I sighed in frustration. "Steven . . ."

"Yes . . ."

"You should be ashamed of yourself, feeding your brother the wrong information. He will grow up, you know."

By the time the real Saturday finally arrived Stedmon was over the top with excitement about getting a new dog. At that point Stedmon's favorite show was "Sponge Bob" while Steven's favorite was "Fresh Prince of Bel Air." Because there was a vast difference in their ages they had few similar interests, so I was hoping a new pet would be a common ground for them both to enjoy.

As we drove to the animal shelter, I reminded the boys that it would require team work to feed, bathe and walk the dog. After each requirement Stedmon said, "I'll do it." I was pleasantly surprised when Steven said, "No problem, Mom," mainly because he often makes his brother do his chores when I'm not around. I was excited to hear that they were willing to work together.

When we arrived at the dog shelter, Stedmon leaped out of the car and shouted, "We're here, Steven! We're here, Steven! Go get the dog."

Steven shook his head. "That's not how it works. We actually get to choose the one we want."

Stedmon shook his head. "I don't want to pick him--you pick him."

Steven reasoned with his brother. "What are you afraid of? The dogs are all in cages. They can't bite you."

Stedmon shook his head, resolute. "I don't want to go. Just go get the dog and bring him to me."

I said, "Stedmon!"

"Yes, Mom?"

"I can't believe what I'm seeing. Since when are you afraid of dogs?"

"I'm not. I just don't want to see them in front of me."

"Give me your hand. If the dog tries to attack you I promise to give him Steven to eat. Deal?"

"Deal" said Stedmon with a big grin on his face. He'd always loved the idea of seeing Steven in trouble.

As soon as we entered the shelter the dogs were barking so loud that Stedmon suddenly bolted for the door. When I caught up with him, he said, "Tell Steven to pick the dog and name her Daisy." I was laughing hard because I could read the fear on his face. I tried to hide my laughter, but it was hard because just the day before he'd been running around the house singing, "I'm going to pick my dog tomorrow."

As I comforted Stedmon, Steven selected a three-month old puppy that was part German shepherd and part Rottweiler--the prettiest puppy I had seen in a long time. Steven tried to coax Stedmon to stroke her back with his hands. And though he did it, he stood a foot away and reached out with cautious deliberation.

The shelter processed the paperwork and soon we took our new puppy home.

In the car Stedmon asked, "Steven, did you name her Daisy?"

"I sure did. Just the way you asked."

"Steven!"

"What is it now?"

"Does she know her name is Daisy?"

Steven sighed aloud. "She will eventually."

"Steven! What does *eventually* mean?"

"It means you have to feed the dog in the morning and walk her every day before I come home from school."

In the mirror I could see Stedmon frown. "I don't want a dog anymore. I feel sad. I feel scared."

Steven shook his head. "Listen, Mom, you know he's only saying that because he doesn't want to feed and walk the dog."

Stedmon argued, "That's not true. It may be part of the reason, but caring for a puppy is a big job for a little guy like me."

I interjected, "Listen, Steven, I know what's going on here. Do you remember when Dad took the training wheels off your bike and you were afraid to ride it?"

"Yes."

"Well, that's the way he's feeling now because it's something new and a little scary for him. He doesn't care for himself. I care for him. In the same way it's a big deal for him to care for a puppy, so please be patient with him. Okay?"

Steven nodded. "Yes, Mom."

"Listen, Stedmon--when you go to bed tonight why don't you talk to Jesus about how you feel so He can help you feel better about your new puppy?"

When we arrived home with Daisy, Stedmon ran straight into his bedroom and crawled under his bunk bed/ play house, and nobody could make him come out. Finally, Steven said, "Stedmon, Daisy is crying because she wants to be your friend. Come and stroke her back so she can stop crying." Stedmon crawled out from under the bed. Once again he stood several feet away and stretched out his hand to stroke her back.

Steven smiled. "You see, Stedmon? She stopped crying. That means she wants to be your friend. Why don't you come and hold her? She won't bite you. She's missing her mom, so she needs you to hold her."

After some serious deliberation Stedmon finally agreed.

As he held Daisy in his lap she rested her head on his arm and shortly went to sleep. Smiling he yelled, "Steven, you're right. She is my friend! She really is my friend!"

Momentarily he turned the puppy around, looked at her face and smiled. "She's my best friend in the whole world."

Steven said, "Well good, because it will be your turn to feed her in the morning."

"No way."

I gave him a reality check. "Listen Stedmon, you promised that if I would let you get a dog, you would help walk, feed, play with and care for her. That's the only way the puppy will become your friend."

He vehemently shook his head. "I don't want any more friends. And I'm not Steven's friend either."

"That's not a nice thing to say. Dogs are amazing. They're loving, fun, playful and trusting. Just like I care for you Daisy needs you to give her food and water and to play with her and walk her. If you love her and take care of her she really will become your best friend. She will even protect you from Steven. How does that sound?"

Stedmon looked at me with a question in his eyes. "Mom?"

"Yes, honey?"

"Do I have to pray about this?"

I nodded. "It wouldn't hurt. But why are you so eager to pray?"

"Well, you make me pray about everything, and I wanted to get it over with because 'Sponge Bob' comes on in thirty minutes."

Stedmon can't tell time. With that in mind I looked at my watch. "You're close. It's actually only twelve minutes before your show comes on so you'd better hurry up and pray. Maybe you could ask God to help you not be afraid of Daisy, because she needs you to be her friend and love her like I love you."

Stedmon's Prayer

"Dear Jesus. I like my new puppy, but I don't want to feed her or walk her. Can you let Daisy not be hungry until Steven comes home from school so he can feed her? Can you make me and Daisy best friends so she will bite Steven when he bothers me? Thank you, Jesus, for my new puppy."

A Mother's Thoughts

"Dear Lord. Today I had to laugh seeing Stedmon run from the dogs at the animal shelter. Although I knew his fear was genuine I want to encourage him to face his fears instead of running from them. I want him to know that no matter how scary life gets God will always be there to give him courage to do the scary things. Help him to feel genuine compassion for Daisy and to learn what it means to have empathy in order to truly care for others. Amen."

EIGHT

The Imagination Station

The majority of fifth grade students have mastered basic reading skills, but others still struggle. At age ten, Stedmon did not struggle to pronounce words or comprehend the stories. He had a unique issue: adding words to the stories that weren't there.

His fourth grade teacher required that all students read at least thirty minutes every night. I thought that sounded like a good thing. I planned to let him choose his own book so he would enjoy what he was reading.

Every night when reading, I would point to the words while he read. He would read those words, but also add words that were not a part of the story. I would say, "Stedmon, where do you see that word?" For example, if the story read "The boy jumped over the wall," he would read, "The boy jumped over the wall and ran very fast." If it said, "Grandpa, please tell us a story," he would say, "Grandpa, please tell us the story about Spiderman." His teacher also noticed this problem and together we decided he needed special help.

I thought it was his eyes, so I had his eyes examined and found that his vision was perfect. When he would add the words to the story. I would stop and ask, "Stedmon, where do you see that word on the paper?" And he would say, "I don't. It just sounds better. After several of these attempts, I sternly said, "Stedmon you are not to read to improve on the book. You are to read the book as it is."

Stedmon Makes Me Laugh and I Make Him Pray

Finally, I had had enough. I felt Stedmon had a serious reading problem, because I could not stop him from reading words that were not on the page. The teacher suggested a reading program as well as a personal tutor.

I was deeply troubled, thinking my son had a serious problem that would prevent him from being a successful reader. I was also beginning to think he might require medical attention since the eye doctor said there was nothing wrong with his eyes and the ear doctor said he could hear just fine.

I mentioned the issue to my sister, Cynthia. "I spoke with Stedmon's teacher today. She recommended a reading skills program for Stedmon. I contacted the Institute of Reading Development and they have a program that will cost a little under $500 for a six-week program. I really think I need to enroll him in this program so he can get some help with his reading problem."

Cynthia frowned. "Sister, that's quite a bit of money."

"But I heard the program had a high success rate. And I've exhausted every other solution."

"Well, go ahead and try it. When are the classes going to be held?"

"Every Saturday."

Steven screamed out from his room. "Stedmon is going to have a problem going on Saturday because that's when he has football practice."

"Well, he'll just have to understand. He needs to stop reading words that are not a part of the story. I am going to enroll him in the program today."

I approached Stedmon with the new plan. "Guess what, Stedmon."

"What?"

"I just enrolled you in a Saturday reading skills programs designed for kids your age and taught by instructors from the Institute for Reading Development."

"Saturday?"

"Yes, every Saturday for six weeks."

Two weeks later I decided to get a progress report from the instructor.

"Miss Jones, how is Stedmon doing? Is he still reading imaginary words?"

Before Miss Jones could answer, Stedmon interrupted and said," I don't do that anymore."

I looked at him and said, "What do you mean that you don't do that anymore?"

Miss Jones said, "I haven't noticed that problem at all. He is successfully reading the stories as they are written."

"Stedmon, how did you do that?"

"Oh, I did it on my own. I don't like adding words any more. Steven said that if I stop reading the extra words I could play football again, so I just stopped. Do I get to go to football practice today?"

"Are you kidding? No way."

Boy, was I angry because I could not get a refund on the $500 I spent to enroll him in the class. I picked up the phone and called Steven.

"Steven. Stedmon is not reading imaginary words anymore."

Steven said, "Well Mom, it sounds like your investment is paying off."

"No, that's not it. It just means I lost $500, after he decided on his own not to add the words, and that means he could have done that a long time ago."

Steven started to laugh.

"I don't see why you're laughing. Your brother is in major trouble."

"Stedmon!"

"Yes, Mom."

"You're grounded until you go to college. You really need to talk to Jesus for a long time on this one."

Stedmon's Prayer

"Dear Jesus, you'd think by now I'd be getting this stuff, but here I am now grounded until college. I'll be an old man before I get out."
"Stedmon!"
"Sorry, Mom. Sorry, Jesus, amen."

A Mother's Thoughts

Dear God, it was a tough pill to swallow knowing I had wasted such a huge sum of money for no good reason, and I'm going to have a talk with Stedmon about the value of money. But I also need to remember that you are the provider of all good things to those who love you, and we're even allowed to waste a little because you love us. Thank you, God for being patient with me, and help me be as patient with my son.

NINE

Clothes Make the Man

At age twenty-one Steven moved into an apartment with his musician friends; and as a frequent visitor at our house he keeps clothes both at his place and ours.

Before Christmas he asked for new clothes in a smaller size because he was eating healthier, trying to lose weight from his stocky build. I purchased several new outfits for him. When he went back to his place he left the hip new clothes, still in their gift boxes, in his old room, until they fit better. His old room had now become a music room, where Stedmon often goes to play drums, keyboard, and a bass guitar.

Sometime later I noticed Stedmon wearing new clothes, and I mentioned it.

He shrugged and said, "Oh, Steven said I could wear them."

I thought nothing of it until a month later when Steven called me on the phone. Stedmon and I were eating dinner at Kentucky Fried Chicken when Steven dropped by the house to try on the clothes, and found that the pants and shirts were smaller and their color had faded. Steven respectfully shouted over the phone, "Mom, why did you let Stedmon wear my new clothes? He washed and shrunk them so they won't fit me anymore."

I frowned feeling terrible. "I'm sorry, Steven. I had no idea he was wearing your clothes without your permission, and I've never known him to do the laundry."

Immediately Stedmon knew we were discussing him. He looked chagrined, knowing the jig was up. I handed the phone to Stedmon and said. "Tell your brother what you did to his new clothes."

"I'm sorry, Steven. I just wanted to wash them so they would be clean when you came home. I had no idea they would shrink." He had clearly used very hot water.

Before I could say another word, Stedmon shrugged and shook his head. "I know. I'm praying."

And of course, I laugh.

Post Script:

In the End

While it may seem as if the boys tricked and plotted against one another as they were growing up, they were actually very protective of each other. Case in point: They could be fighting like cats and dogs, but the moment I corrected one of them the other would defend him. The bond, though unusual, is strong, even now.

Today Steven is twenty-three and Stedmon is thirteen, and the two get along famously. They are very well-mannered and have a strong faith in God. Steven is a full-time music minister who spends a good deal of time in a music studio, playing and recording his arrangements, which puts Stedmon in even greater awe of him. Steven is very laid back and worries about nothing, which is why he has a growing collection of parking tickets.

Stedmon is now in middle school and is still as cagey and hilarious as ever. It's not that he tries to be funny, and in fact, he doesn't seem to know he's funny—it's just the way he looks at life. I trust that God is doing a good work in my boys, so that, most important of all, they bring Him glory.

A MOTHER'S FINAL THOUGHTS

If you've read this far you know that over the years Stedmon often got into trouble and was told to go talk to Jesus. And while that may have seemed like punishment at the time, it has turned out to be a good thing, actually developing him into a young man of consistent prayer.

These days he discusses everything with God, and, in the process, makes his mother a happy woman, because I know he'll be fine as long as he prays.

Stedmon and Steven

At the time of this writing Stedmon is age 13 and Steven, age 23.

CPSIA information can be obtained at www.ICGtesting.com
Printed in the USA
LVOW110533080512

280728LV00004B/1/P